Classics for Keyboard
Thirty world-famous pieces
arranged by Keith Stent

Kevin Mayhew

We hope you enjoy the music in *Classics for Keyboard.*
Further copies are available from your local music shop.

In case of difficulty, please contact the publisher direct:

The Sales Department
KEVIN MAYHEW LTD
Rattlesden
Bury St Edmunds
Suffolk IP30 0SZ

Phone 01449 737978
Fax 01449 737834

Please ask for our complete catalogue of outstanding Instrumental Music.

Front Cover: *Moss roses, peonies and double hollyhocks*
by Johan Laurentz Jensen (1800-1856).
Reproduced by kind permission of Verner Amell Ltd/
Fine Art Photographic Library, London

Cover designed by Juliette Clarke and Graham Johnstone.
Picture Research: Jane Rayson

First published in Great Britain in 1995 by Kevin Mayhew Ltd

ISBN 0 86209 609 X
Catalogue No: 3611139

All or part of these pieces have been arranged by Keith Stent
and are the copyright of Kevin Mayhew Ltd.

Music Editor: Donald Thomson
Music setting by Kevin Whomes

Printed and bound in Great Britain

Contents

TRUMPET VOLUNTARY

Jeremiah Clarke (c.1674 - 1707)

5

STUDY IN A MINOR

Friedrich Burgmüller (1806 - 1874)

ANDANTE

Cornelius Gurlitt (1820 - 1901)

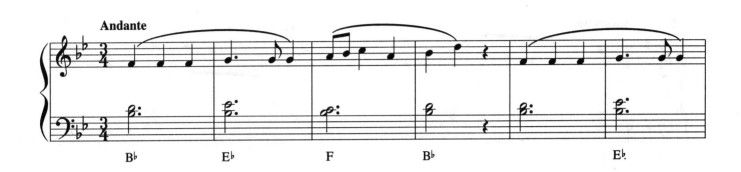

TWO MINUETS FOR MRS BACH

Johann Sebastian Bach (1685 - 1750)

II   Allegretto

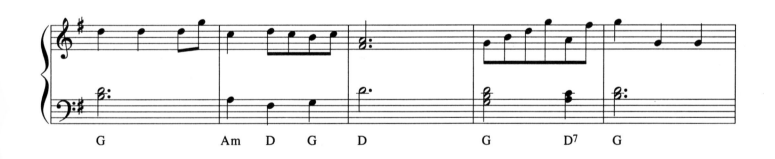

QUESTION AND ANSWER

Samuel Coleridge-Taylor (1875 - 1912)

TAMBOURIN

François-Joseph Gossec (1734 - 1829)

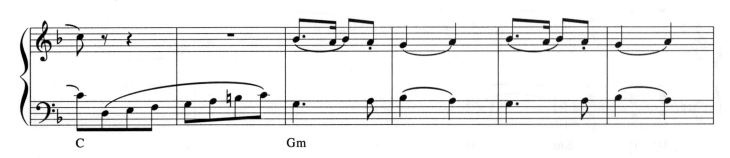

SPRING from 'The Four Seasons'

Antonio Vivaldi (1678 - 1741)

SLUMBER SONG

Franz Schubert (1797 - 1828)

LIEBESTRAUM

Franz Liszt (1811 - 1886)

MINUET IN G

Ludwig van Beethoven (1770 - 1827)

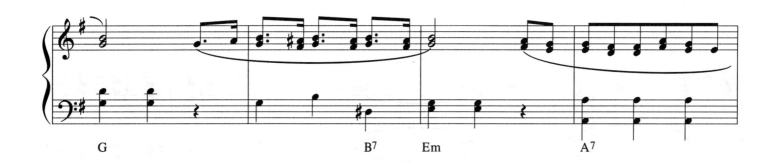

19

PAVANE

Gabriel Fauré (1845 - 1924)

AUTUMN from 'The Four Seasons'

Antonio Vivaldi (1678 - 1741)

GYMNOPÉDIE I

Erik Satie (1866 - 1925)

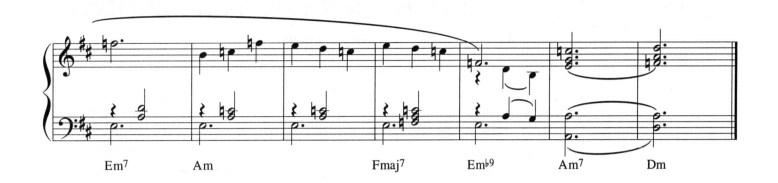

PRELUDE

Alexander Scriabin (1872 - 1915)

THE FLOWERS THAT BLOOM IN THE SPRING

Arthur Sullivan (1842 - 1900)

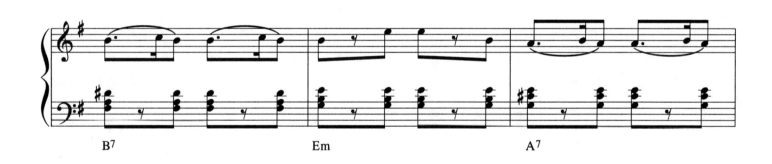

Am　　　　　　　D　　　　　　　Am

D　　　　　　　G

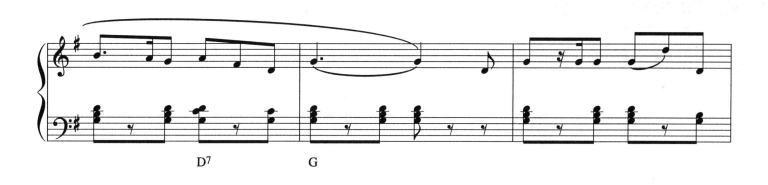

D⁷　　　　　　G

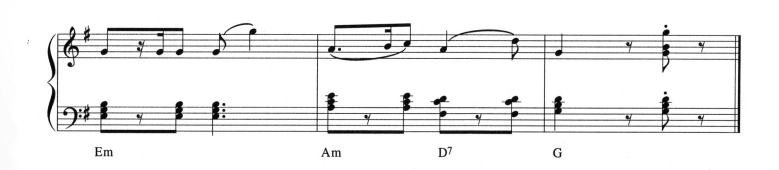

Em　　　　　　Am　　D⁷　　　G

ALLEGRO NON TROPPO

Anton Diabelli (1781 - 1853)

LARGO from 'Serse'

George Frideric Handel (1685 - 1759)

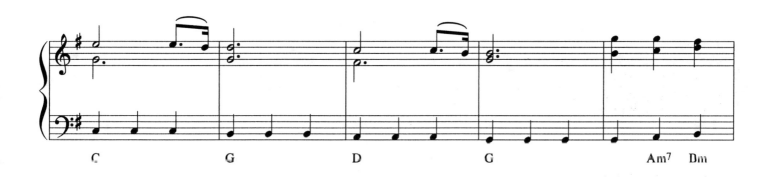

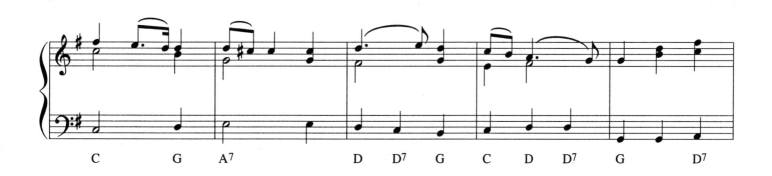

GAVOTTE

Carl Reinecke (1824 - 1910)

BAGATELLE

Anton Diabelli (1781 - 1853)

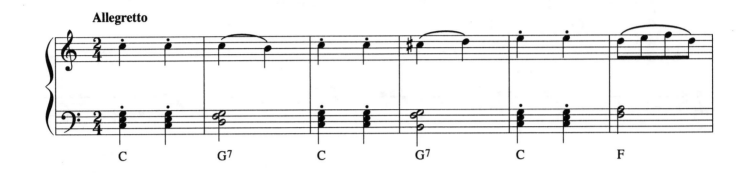

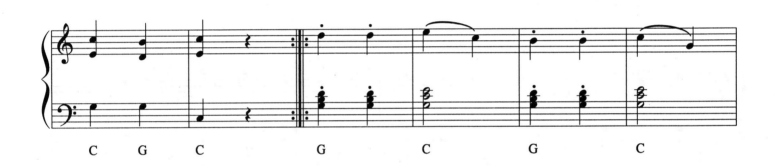

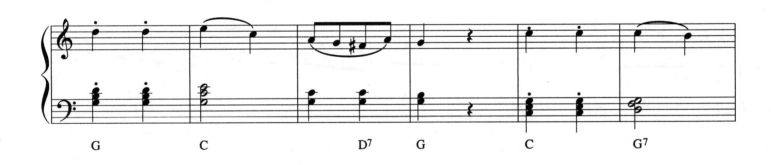

THE MERRY PEASANT

Robert Schumann (1810 - 1856)

TURKISH RONDO from Sonata K331

Wolfgang Amadeus Mozart (1756 - 1791)

33

NOCTURNE

Frédéric Chopin (1810 - 1849)

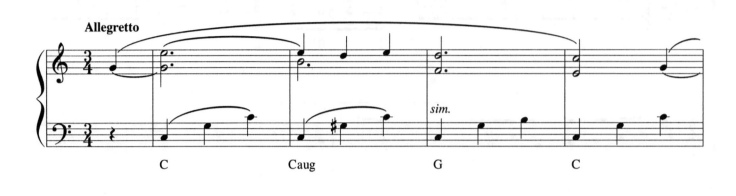

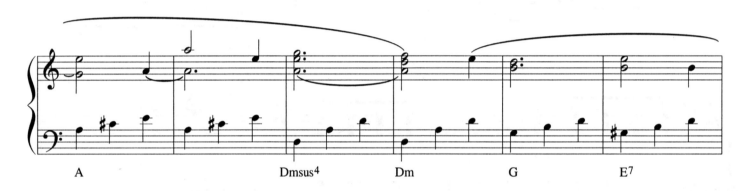

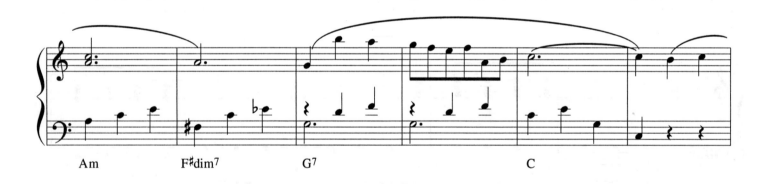

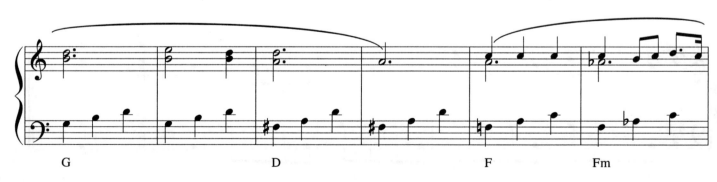

35

SLEIGH RIDE

Wolfgang Amadeus Mozart (1756 - 1791)

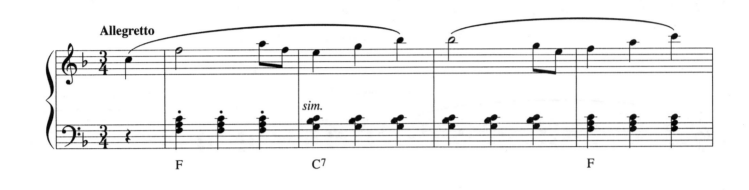

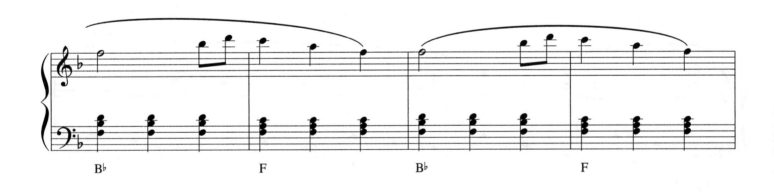

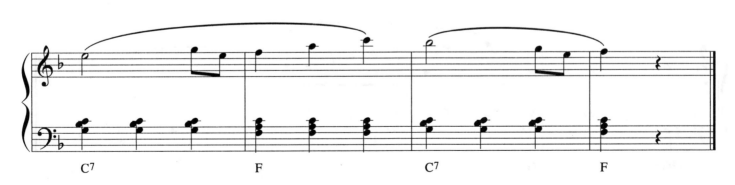

THE WILD HORSEMAN

Robert Schumann (1810 - 1856)

ALLEGRO AND VIVACE from Sonatina in C

Muzio Clementi (1752 - 1832)

G   Cm   G   G⁷   Cm

G   Cm   G   C

G   G⁷   C

G   C   G   C

G⁷   C   F   G⁷   C

41

MORNING from 'Peer Gynt'

Edvard Grieg (1843 - 1907)

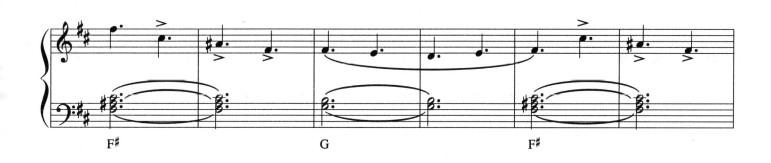

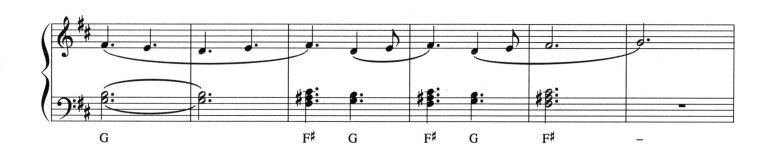

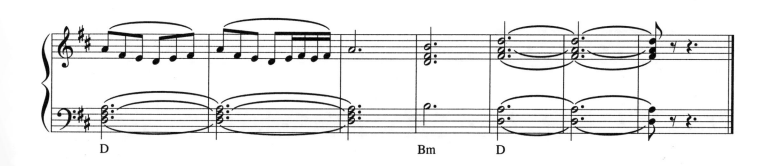

SKATERS' WALTZ

Emile Waldteufel (1837 - 1915)

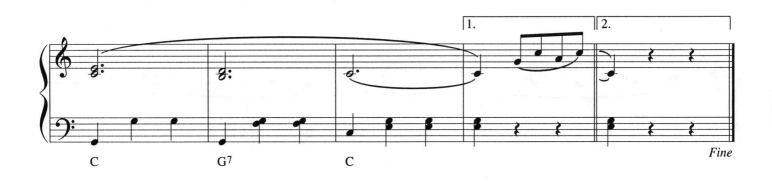

45

SARABANDE

George Frideric Handel (1685 - 1759)

GERMAN DANCE

Franz Schubert (1797 - 1828)

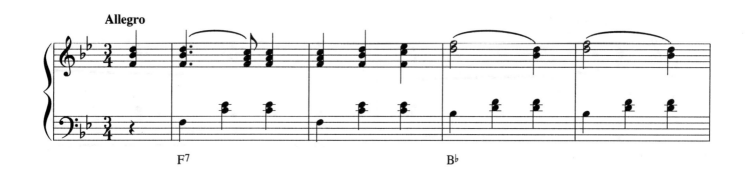

ÉCOSSAISE

Ludwig van Beethoven (1770 - 1827)

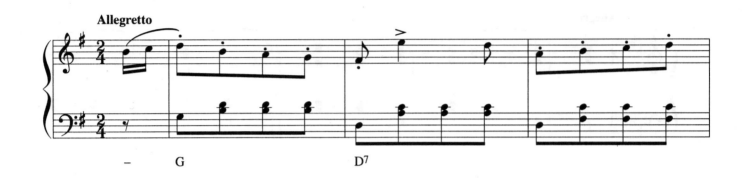

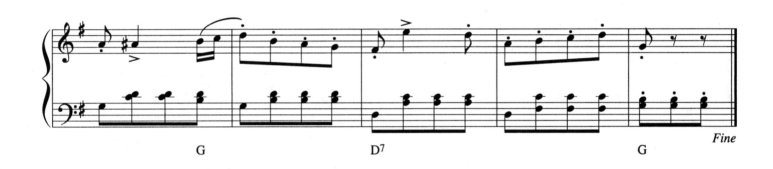

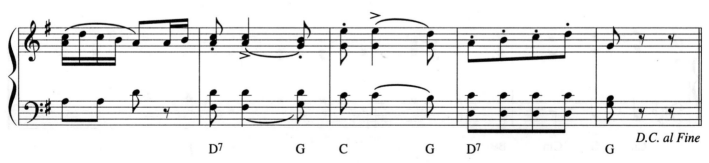